THE FRIEND I NEED

BEING KIND & CARING TO MYSELF

by Gabi Garcia
illustrated by
Miranda Rivadeneira

Some days are hard.
Today was one of those days. At school, I didn't pass my spelling test even though I practiced the words all week.

"I'm never going to learn."

On the way home, I kept falling off my bicycle and scraped my knee.

"Everyone else can do it except me."

Later, I spilled milk all over my artwork. "Why am I so clumsy? It's ruined!" I crumpled the painting and snapped at Sofia for leaving her cup on the table.

It's tough being a kid sometimes.
My thoughts and words can be mean.
It feels yucky. I need a friend.

I've spent a lot of time learning and practicing how to be a friend to others.

But what does it mean to be a friend to myself?

A friend is there for you.
When Dara was frustrated and threw her jump rope on the ground at recess because she kept getting tangled, I sat by her side. I listened and waited until she was ready to play again.

When I'm angry, disappointed, or having another strong emotion, I don't have to pretend I'm not upset. I can pay attention to what's happening and sit with what I'm feeling until I'm ready to figure out what I need.

A friend is understanding and kind.

When Santi almost quit dance class because he couldn't follow along with the moves, I encouraged him to keep trying. I reminded him that it takes time to learn new things and that we all mess up sometimes.

When I mess up or things don't go the way I hoped, I can talk to myself the way I'd talk to a friend. Supportive words hold me up when I'm having a tough time.

These are some I can try:

I tried my best.

It's okay to feel this way.

I am worthy of love and kindness even when I mess up.

I'm not perfect, and I don't need to be.

I forgive myself.

I can be my own friend.

I can also give myself a hug,

hold my own hand,

or find another gentle touch if that's what I need.

This can help me feel safe and calm.

A friend is honest and wants what's best for you.

When Malik wanted to sneak in extra screen time during our playdate, I said no and suggested an activity his parents would be okay with instead.

Being honest with myself means taking responsibility if my words or actions hurt someone.

It means I work to make things better and forgive myself for my mistakes.

When I stand up for something I believe in, let others know what I need, or ask for help, I'm doing what's best for me.

A friend makes time for things you like to do.

Drawing,

listening to music,

spending time with friends,

or being outside are a few activities I enjoy.

Making time for these activities is a way to show kindness and care for myself.

After yelling at Sofia, I ran into my room. My chin trembled and I collapsed into a puddle of tears. I was a snotty mess, but it was okay.

I found a breath deep in my belly and sat with my feelings. I thought about what a friend would need to hear and said those words to myself. Even though what I did was wrong, I know I'm a caring person. I reminded myself that everybody has bad days. I forgave myself.

I was the friend I needed.

Then I apologized to Sofia for what I did and told her I wanted to make things better. She accepted my apology and asked if I wanted to work on an art project. Together.

When I make a mistake or things don't go the way I hoped, I can talk to myself the way I'd talk to a friend.

What would you like to hear when you're having a tough time? What would feel encouraging or comforting to hear? If this is hard, imagine what you'd say to a friend in this situation.

Write it down and read it to yourself whenever you need.

GENTLE TOUCHES

Did you know you can offer comfort to yourself with a gentle touch? It can help you feel **safe** and **connected** when you're having a tough time. Some examples of gentle touches include:

- giving yourself a hug
- placing both hands on your heart
- holding your hand

Take a deep breath and give them a try. Decide what feels good to you.

Being the friend I need helps me remember that I matter just the way I am.

It helps me sit with the difficult feelings I experience with kindness.

Treating myself with love and understanding helps me learn from my mistakes so I can try again.

Practicing forgiveness helps me take responsibility for my words and actions.

IT MAKES ME A BETTER FRIEND TO OTHERS TOO.

PARENTS & EDUCATORS

It's tough being a kid sometimes. The pressures they feel are real. Unfortunately, so is the negative self-talk that can sometimes follow when children don't get things right the first time (or the fifth) or when emotions are strong. But it doesn't have to be this way.

Most children have probably spent time in school or at home learning how to be good friends to others, but what about being good friends to themselves?

The Friend I Need helps children understand that the same qualities they look for in a friend-- someone who is kind, understanding, forgiving, wants what's best for them, etc., they can offer to themselves. This is especially important for them to do when they're having a hard time.

Instead of being mean to themselves or minimizing their actions when they make mistakes or things do not go the way they wanted, children can learn to forgive themselves and to speak to themselves with kindness and understanding. This is a process that doesn't happen overnight, but when children learn to put these concepts into practice, they are more likely to try again when they make a mistake, ask for help when they need it, or apologize for their words or actions when they've been hurtful.

The Friend I Need also introduces children to the practice of giving themselves gentle touches to soothe themselves. A caring touch such as hugging themselves or holding their own hand can make them feel safe and connected. While it might take practice and some getting used to, it can be a powerful tool.

When children learn to be friends to themselves, they are valuing their needs and their feelings so they can offer care and kindness to themselves when they need it. The Friend I Need offers a springboard for parents, educators, and caregivers to have conversations about what it means to be a friend to themselves.

You can continue to support your child in this process by helping them identify and name what they're feeling, by validating whatever they feel, and by normalizing mistakes. We live in an achievement-oriented society and children need to know that they are loved, valued and appreciated just as they are.

Keep in mind that children learn by observation, so it's important for you to practice and model being a friend to yourself too.

Warmly,
Gabi

Hi, I'm Gabi.

Thank you for choosing this book. I'm a mama, children's book author, and licensed professional counselor. I spent 21 years learning from the children I worked with in the public schools, something I am immensely grateful for. These experiences, along with just being a human on this planet, inspire the books I write.

I believe in the power and beauty of books. I hope that the ones I write will be of service to parents, educators, and other caregivers, and of course children, and contribute in some small way toward making this world a better place. You can find out more on my website: gabigarciabooks.com.

If you found this book useful, I would sincerely appreciate your honest review! It's one of the best ways to help others find it.

OTHER BOOKS BY GABI GARCIA

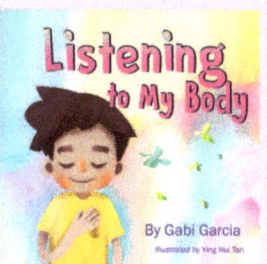 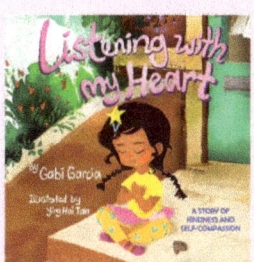   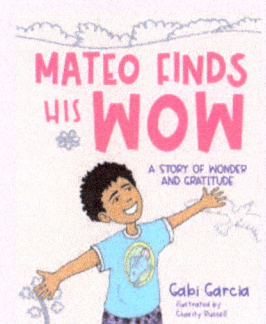

ALL TITLES AVAILABLE IN SPANISH

Hi, I'm Miranda.

I'm a graphic designer and illustrator. A lover of books, colors, typography, and shape.

When someone tells me a story, I imagine it in my head as a melody that is translated into images and colors.

What I like most about my profession is that it allows me to recreate the world, tell new things and express them in a different way. I like being part of that transformation.

Visit mirandarivadeneira.com.ar to find out more.

MAY WE ALL LEARN TO BE THE FRIEND WE NEED

Publisher's Cataloging-in-Publication Data
Names: Garcia, Gabi, author. | Rivadeneira, Miranda, illustrator.
Title: The friend I need : being kind & caring to myself / by Gabi Garcia ; illustrated by Miranda Rivadeneira.
Description: Austin, TX: Skinned Knee Publishing , 2020. | Summary: A young boy is having a hard day and learns that he can be be a kind friend to himself.
Identifiers: ISBN: 978-1-949633-23-8 (Hardcover); 978-1-949633-19-1 (pbk.); 978-1-949633-20-7 (e-book)
Subjects: LCSH Self-acceptance--Juvenile literature. | Mindfulness--Juvenile literature. | Failure (Psychology) in children--Juvenile literature. | Friendship--Juvenile literature. | Emotions--Juvenile literature. | CYAC Self-acceptance. | Mindfulness. | Failure (Psychology) in children. | Friendship. | Emotions. | BISAC JUVENILE NONFICTION / Social Topics / Emotions & Feelings | JUVENILE NONFICTION / Social Topics / Self-Esteem & Self-Reliance | JUVENILE NONFICTION / Social Topics / Friendship
Classification: LCC BJ1533.S27 .G37 2020| DDC 158/.1--dc23

Copyright © 2020 by
Gabi Garcia Books, LLC
All rights reserved.
gabigarciabooks.com

skinned knee
publishing
902 Gardner Road no. 4
Austin, Texas 78721

www.ingramcontent.com/pod-product-compliance
Lightning Source LLC
Chambersburg PA
CBHW041216240426
43661CB00012B/1062